Strategic Leadership for Sustainable Personal and Organizational Success

Dr. Mason Oghenejobo

Copyright © 2014 Dr. Mason Oghenejobo.

All rights reserved. No part of this book may be used or reproduced by any means, graphic, electronic, or mechanical, including photocopying, recording, taping or by any information storage retrieval system without the written permission of the publisher except in the case of brief quotations embodied in critical articles and reviews.

Scripture quotations taken from the Holy Bible, New Living Translation, Copyright © 1996, 2004. Used by permission of Tyndale House Publishers, Inc., Wheaton, Illinois 60189. All rights reserved.

Scripture taken from the *Amplified Bible*, copyright © 1954, 1958, 1962, 1964, 1965, 1987 by The Lockman Foundation. Used by permission.

Scripture taken from the New King James Version. Copyright © 1979, 1980, 1982 by Thomas Nelson, Inc. Used by permission. All rights reserved.

WestBow Press books may be ordered through booksellers or by contacting:

WestBow Press
A Division of Thomas Nelson & Zondervan
1663 Liberty Drive
Bloomington, IN 47403
www.westbowpress.com
1 (866) 928-1240

Because of the dynamic nature of the Internet, any web addresses or links contained in this book may have changed since publication and may no longer be valid. The views expressed in this work are solely those of the author and do not necessarily reflect the views of the publisher, and the publisher hereby disclaims any responsibility for them.

Any people depicted in stock imagery provided by Thinkstock are models, and such images are being used for illustrative purposes only. Certain stock imagery © Thinkstock.

ISBN: 978-1-4908-5165-5 (sc)
ISBN: 978-1-4908-5166-2 (hc)
ISBN: 978-1-4908-5164-8 (e)

Library of Congress Control Number: 2014916550

Printed in the United States of America.

WestBow Press rev. date: 11/26/2014

To my wonderful wife, Vivian, our children, our grandchildren, and all who have—through their instructions, writings, actions, and reactions—taught me that strategic leadership is a life skill that enables people and organizations that understand and practice it to flourish in our complex world.

Contents

Introduction .... **ix**

Chapter 1: Strategic Leadership Overview 1
Chapter 2: Personal Leadership Poverty 12
Chapter 3: The Leader as Light:
A Concept for Developing
Global Leaders 34
Chapter 4: Leadership Theories and Practices 46
Chapter 5: Power and Influence 74
Chapter 6: Coaching, Counseling,
Mentoring, and Discipling 82
Chapter 7: Organizational Theories and
Practices 93
Chapter 8: Personal and Organizational
Renewal 104

Endnotes **111**
About the Author **117**

Introduction

Leadership takes place at three levels—personal, team/organizational, and societal. Although the complexities of the capabilities required for leadership success increase as you move from the personal to the organizational and societal levels, it is the quality of the "self" (personal values, character and competences) that determines if a leader will succeed or not. In fact, most leadership failures occur at the personal level. For example, according to Scott Roberts of PinkNews,[1] the CEO of a major oil and gas company lost his position because he lied about an inappropriate relationship he had with a male suitor. Also, according to Jennifer Peltz and Tom Hayes (AP),[2] a former IMF CEO resigned because of a case of attempted rape. Moreover, CNN International[3] stated that a former US president almost lost his position as the president of the United States of America because of his affair with an intern, which the president himself described as a "terrible moral error."

These were reported cases of personal leadership failures. We learn from these and several other cases that leadership development starts from personal values development. Leadership is what you do to yourself first, before you do it with others. If the "self" qualities are deficient, then the leader suffers from personal leadership poverty, and he will be unsuccessful. He therefore needs mentoring, coaching, discipling, renewal, and/or other interventions to overcome his personal leadership poverty.

A review of biblical leaders and followers who succeeded or failed in their personal and organizational leadership responsibilities has revealed seven key characteristics that leaders who suffer from personal leadership poverty need to address to become successful. These are the lack of: (1) the true God, (2) physical and emotional health, (3) good character and integrity, (4) requisite competence, (5) good human relationships, (6) physical and spiritual security, and (7) financial stewardship. Assessing and developing leaders to overcome these potential deficiencies will enable them to exhibit righteous love, build trust and good relationships that are essential in building transformative organizations. In this book, the key elements of the personal leadership poverty framework and strategic leadership are elaborated with several examples that will help leaders and organizations overcome their leadership challenges and subsequently thrive.

The book starts with an overview of strategic leadership, which clarifies the essence of leadership, strategy, and management. This is followed by a discussion on personal leadership poverty, which elaborates the personal leadership framework and how leaders can improve their overall leadership capabilities and practices. The tenets of global leadership are encapsulated in the chapter titled "The Leader as Light." The chapter on leadership theories and practices provides insight into leadership theories, concepts, and models that enhance leadership practices. The chapter on power and influence provides insight into types and sources of power, influence tactics, and how humans respond to the use of power and influence in leader-follower relationships.

The book emphasizes that it is difficult to solve complex problems, serve large numbers of customers, or develop societies without organizations, where people with diverse capabilities work to achieve common organizational purposes. Interestingly, the quality of an organization is determined by the quality of its people. Hence, leadership-followership development, succession planning and management are essential for organizational survival and growth.

In chapter 6, I discuss coaching, counseling, mentoring and discipling, which highlight the concepts of collaborative/facilitative leadership and provide some of the methods organizations can use to develop their leaders and followers.

Chapter 7 discusses organizational theories and practices, organizational design, organizational learning, creativity/innovation, and organizational trustworthiness, which provide insight into how organizations can be designed/re-configured and led to sustainably thrive.

Finally, the book ends with a discussion on personal and organizational renewal, which highlights how leaders can continuously renew themselves and their organizations to thrive even after they fail, fall, or suffer setbacks.

I pray that this book helps to improve your leadership capabilities and practices.

Dr. Mason Oghenejobo

Chapter 1

Strategic Leadership Overview

The challenges we face today cannot be solved with the same kind of thinking that was used when they were created.

—Albert Einstein

According to M. E. Porter, the two key factors that contribute to sustainable superior performance in organizations are operational excellence and strategy.[1] Consequently, while operational excellence is essential and critical to organizational success, it is insufficient to sustain competitive advantage. On the other hand, strategy alone without operational excellence will not lead to sustainable superior performance, as a strategy that is not operationalized or implemented is a failed strategy. According to Porter, strategy entails deliberately choosing a different set of activities and positioning a firm to deliver a unique mix of value that provides sustainable competitive advantage. R. A. Burgelman asserts that strategy is about "winning" sustainably in the midst of change. It is synonymous to destiny creation and realization amid change.[2] Burgelman defines destiny as achieving a predetermined state through right choices and actions. This is contrary to the fatalistic concept of destiny as a predetermined outcome of events that occur irrespective of what people or organizations do.

Why is strategy critical in achieving sustainable superior performance in organizations? Strategy is essential because we live in a world characterized by:

- **Complexity.** Organizations have to deal with diverse, autonomous, interdependent, intricately linked, and interrelated persons, organizations, and units (internally and externally) in order to deliver value, survive, and thrive.
- **Conflicts and Chaos.** Divergent interests and actions create conflicts that may lead to chaos and crises that organizations and their employees have to deal with. In fact, most challenges that organizations face can be framed as conflicts. Consequently, harnessing and managing conflicts have become a life skill that persons and organizations require in order to thrive.

- **Competition and Cooperation.** Organizations have to compete as well as cooperate and form strategic alliances, sometimes with their competitors, in order to thrive.
- **Change.** This can be sudden, continuous, discontinuous, dynamic, and rapid. These changes are driven by technological, socio-cultural, political, economic, demographic, and other factors.
- **Ambiguity.** Some of the challenges that persons and organizations currently face are ill-defined or not well understood, or may have multiple meanings or interpretations. Also, their solutions are not known. Hence, they are ambiguous and seem "mysterious."
- **Paradox.** Some of the challenges that organizations grapple with and their potential solutions are paradoxical—they appear contradictory or absurd, yet they are true or are derived from facts; their meaning and solutions seem to contradict commonly accepted opinions or beliefs, yet they are true. For example, the statement by our Lord Jesus Christ that "it is more blessed to give than to receive" (Acts 20:35 NKJV) is paradoxical. A poor person or organization that is in need of money may consider the

statement absurd, yet it is true. Also, the Bible teaches us that "there is one that scatters, yet increases more. And there is one that withholds more than is right, but it leads to poverty" (Prov. 11:24 NKJV). These biblical statements indicate that the limitations of our current thinking and mental schemata may be the reason why we consider some seemingly paradoxical and creative solutions that we are offered, as absurd or not feasible. Consequently, deep reflections and the renewing of our minds are essential for "times of refreshing" to come into our lives and organizations (Acts 3:19 NKJV).

- **Perplexity.** Organizations are usually stunned or puzzled by the differences in socio-cultural, economic, infrastructural, security, and political challenges they face as they attempt to enter different countries.
- **Temptation.** Leaders who are powerful and wealthy attract temptations. Several biblical and contemporary leaders failed because of temptations and moral bankruptcy. For example, Solomon failed because of pagan women.
- **Imperfections.** No human or organization is perfect. Organizations have to work with

imperfect humans, societies, regulations, data/information, systems, and processes in order to thrive.
- **Irony.** When what is said or what is expected turns out to be unreal or opposite, what should leaders and organizations do? When leaders and organizations see "servants on horses, while princes walk on the ground like servants" (Eccl. 10:7 NKJV), what should they do?
- **Spiritual and Invisible Battles.** The Bible teaches us that "the things which are seen are temporary, but the things which are not seen eternal" (2 Cor. 4:18 NKJV); that we should be sober (exercise self-control and handle with all seriousness) and be vigilant because our adversary, the Devil (an invisible spirit with his hosts of demons) walks about like a roaring lion, seeking whom he may devour (1 Peter 5:8 AMP). How should leaders and organizations fight spiritual and invisible warfare?

Given a world characterized by complexity, conflict, chaos, competition, selective inclusions/exclusions, change, ambiguity, paradox, perplexity, temptation, imperfections, irony, and spiritual/invisible battles, leaders and organizations require a framework, a way of thinking and doing, that will enable them to survive and thrive; hence, the need for strategy and strategic leadership.

What are the differences between management, leadership, and strategic leadership?

Management is required essentially for operational excellence. It focuses on the efficient and effective use of mainly physical resources (money, materials, machines, methods) to deliver products and services to meet current customer needs. Its outlook is short-term. It tends to treat all humans as the same, essentially like machines. It entails planning (allocating and scheduling resources), organizing, controlling, coordinating, directing, immediate problem solving, and decision making. Management is essentially transactional as it involves making exchanges for work done or results achieved.

Generally, leadership focuses more on people to make things work or get results. It appreciates the psycho-emotional, socio-cultural, and spiritual aspects of humans and consequently treats each person as different. Leadership builds up people rather than tear them down. It entails having positive motives toward others, instituting values, expressing moral/righteous love (tough love), caring, coaching, mentoring, and discipling. It is transactional and transformational.

Strategic leadership is required to ensure sustainable superior performance. It focuses on "creative destruction"—ushering in the new while getting rid of the old; it strives to understand the external and enable the internal to change so as to thrive as the external changes; it anticipates and solves future problems today, so that organizations are well-prepared for the future as it emerges. It entails visioning/direction setting, creativity/innovation, driving changes, harnessing conflicts, succession planning/management, followership development, strategic thinking, strategic planning, and strategy implementation.

Overall, strategic leadership encompasses management, general leadership, and strategy. It enables people and organizations to thrive in the present and future amid dynamic global changes.

Achieving Operational Excellence and Sustainable Superior Performance

You need good management and general leadership to achieve operational excellence. You require strategic leadership to achieve sustainable superior performance.

Achieving Operational Excellence	Achieving Sustainable Superior Performance
Management • Makes things work efficiently and effectively to solve current problems. • Focuses on physical resources (money, materials, machines, methods). • Treats all humans as the same, essentially like machines. • Is short-term in outlook. • Does not anticipate or respond appropriately to changes. • Is essentially transactional. It entails: ➤ planning (scheduling and appropriate allocation of resources) ➤ organizing ➤ coordinating ➤ directing (which is different from direction setting) ➤ solving immediate problems ➤ immediate decision making.	**Strategic Leadership** • Anticipates and solves current and future problems in order to sustain superior performance. • Focuses on destroying the old and creating the new (creative destruction) in order to continuously thrive at all times. • Strives to understand the external and enable the internal to be nimble so that it can appropriately respond to external changes. • Initiates and drives changes. • Appropriately handles and harnesses conflicts. • Develops and grows organizational capability to overcome present and future challenges.

General Leadership	It entails:
<ul><li>Focuses on people/followers to make things work and deliver goods and services.</li><li>Appreciates the psycho-emotional, sociocultural, and spiritual aspects of humans and consequently treats each person as different.</li><li>Builds people up rather tearing them down.</li></ul> It entails:<ul><li>instituting values, expressing moral love (tough love), caring, coaching, mentoring, and discipling</li></ul>	<ul><li>instituting values</li><li>visioning and direction setting</li><li>creativity and innovation</li><li>driving changes</li><li>harnessing conflicts</li><li>succession planning/management</li><li>followership development</li><li>organizational capability development</li><li>strategic thinking</li><li>strategic planning</li><li>strategy implementation</li></ul> Overall, strategic leadership encompasses management, general leadership, and strategy. It enables people and organizations to thrive in the present and future amid dynamic global changes.

How should organizations develop the leadership/ management capabilities of staff as they come in and grow within their organizations?

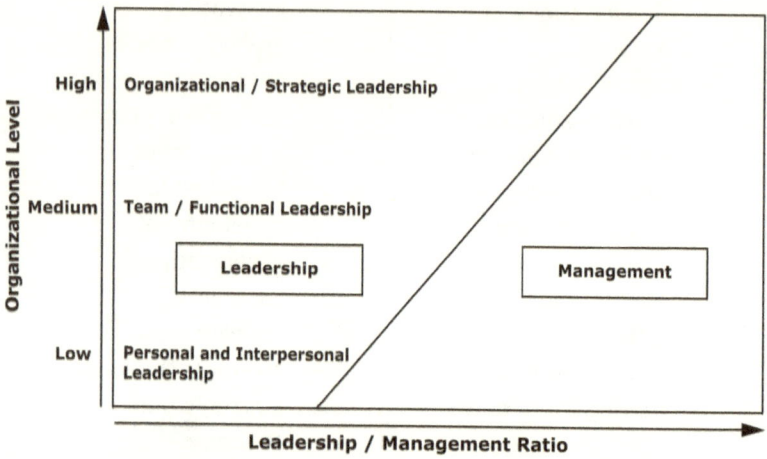

Figure 1: Leadership/Management Capabilities Development Frame

At the entry/low levels of organizations, leadership development should focus mainly on personal leadership and moral/ethical character formation. Staff at this level should be trained to become grounded in their functions and how to properly use, harness, and manage functional resources (processes, procedures, tools/equipment/ materials, funds, etc.). At the middle-manpower level, as they move into team/functional unit leadership positions, they should acquire team leadership capabilities and balance between leadership and management. At the senior levels, the focus should be on strategic leadership, with some management capabilities to ensure business delivery.

Chapter 2

Personal Leadership Poverty

But God said to him, Fool! This night your soul will be required of you; then whose will those things be which you have provided? So is he who lays treasure for himself and is not rich toward God.
—Luke 12:20-21 NKJV

I know your works, tribulation, and poverty (but you are rich).
—Revelation 2:9 NKJV

Because you say, I am rich, have become wealthy, and have need for nothing—and do not know that you are wretched, miserable, poor, blind and naked.
—Revelation 3:17 NKJV

Humans use mainly financial status to assess the richness of a person. Some Christians (like those who were in Laodicea; see Rev. 3:17) believe that being financially and materially wealthy is an indication of spiritual blessings, but this is not true. We learn from the above scriptures that being rich in God's eyes entails far more than financial well-being.

The Chambers Dictionary defines poverty as a state of lack, deficiency, need, or meagerness. Leadership takes place at three levels—personal, team/organizational, and societal. It starts from personal leadership. It is the quality of the "self" that the leader brings to a leadership position that determines if he or she will succeed or not. If the "self" qualities are deficient, then the leader suffers from personal leadership poverty, and he or she will be unsuccessful. The leader therefore needs mentoring, coaching, discipling, and/or other interventions to overcome his or her personal leadership poverty.

What is leadership?

B. Winston asserts that leadership starts from values, and it is expressed in relationships. It entails relating with others with moral love (doing the right things in the right way/manner at the right time) in order to achieve set purposes.[1] Kouzes and Posner describe leadership as a one-to-one (dyadic) or one-to-many relationship that enables the pursuit and achievement of a set purpose, vision, and goals.[2] According to Blanchard and Hodges, leaders and followers bring their **H**earts (motive/love of others), **H**eads (beliefs/theories in use), **H**ands (actions), and **H**abits (daily display of commitment/interests) to all leadership settings. Leadership entails harnessing the **4H** of humans to achieve a set purpose or requisite results.[3] According to R. Rardin, "leadership is an inside-out phenomenon. What is in the heart of the leader gets expressed in his or her words."[4] The Bible also teaches us that "out of the abundance of the heart, the mouth speaks" (Matt. 12:34 NKJV) and "as a man thinks in his heart, so he is" (Prov. 23:7 NKJV).

Overall, leadership is a complex phenomenon of the heart that plays out in relationships that are essential to achieving required results. It is critical to success because individuals cannot achieve much by themselves in their personal lives, in organizations, or in society.

In what aspects do humans exhibit leadership poverty, and how can they overcome it? A review of biblical leaders and followers who succeeded or failed in their personal and organizational leadership responsibilities has revealed seven key characteristics that leaders who suffer from personal leadership poverty need to address to become successful. These are the lack of:

1. The true God.
2. Physical and emotional health.
3. Good character and integrity.
4. Requisite competence.
5. Good human relationships.
6. Physical and spiritual security.
7. Financial stewardship.

Assessing and developing leaders to overcome these potential deficiencies is a strategic activity that will enable them to exhibit righteous love, build trust and good relationships, which are essential in building transformative organizations. The key components of the personal leadership poverty framework are illustrated with biblical examples. Let us start by looking at leadership and the true God.

Leadership and the true God

I refer to the God of the Bible, who created the universe and man, as the true God. He is the God that Jesus Christ served and called His Father. He is the Head of the Holy Trinity (God the Father, God the Son, and God the Holy Spirit) that collectively agreed to "let us make man in Our image, according to Our likeness" (Gen. 1:26 NKJV). Rardin described the Holy Trinity as a model of "shared authority" or partnership and asserted that leadership as a partnership of humans to collectively serve themselves and a common purpose emanates from this model. He asserts that all authority comes from God because the "earth is the Lord's and all its fullness" (Ps. 24:1 NKJV) and God gave man the responsibility and authority "to tend and to keep" the earth (Gen. 2:15 NKJV). Thus, we see that the authority to rightly manage earthly resources and lead humans well in the management and distribution of these earthly resources comes from God. Therefore, all leaders must be accountable to God. Also, through the Ten Commandments and expressions of God's likes/dislikes as recorded in the Bible, God gave man a moral code that should guide our leadership (our relationships with Him and our fellow humans) as we exercise our authority on earth. Love for God and man summarizes the moral code that God gave man to guide his conduct in all relationships. Jesus explained this when He said,

And you shall love the Lord your God with all your heart, with all your soul and with all your mind. This is the first and great commandment. And the second is like it. You shall love your neighbor as yourself. On these two commandments hang all the Law and the Prophets. (Matt. 22:37–40 NKJV)

God asked us to have dominion over physical things, not our fellow humans. We are to love and serve fellow humans. Given that love is an issue of the heart, we find that leadership starts from the heart, and a leader who does not know or relate with the true God or whose heart is not aligned with His will and moral code will eventually fail. According to Blanchard and Hodges, transforming a leader to become successful is a four-stage journey that starts with the leader. It progresses from personal leadership (stage 1) to one-to-one leadership (stage 2) to team/family leadership (stage 3) and subsequently to organizational/community leadership (stage 4). Successful personal leadership development starts and ends with knowing, obeying, and following the true God. Successful biblical leaders like Joseph, David, Nehemiah, Mordecai, Daniel, and Paul did so. Unsuccessful ones like Ahab, Jezebel, and Nebuchadnezzar did otherwise. In fact, the Bible records several nations and groups (e.g., Sodom/Gomorrah and Babylon) that were destroyed because their leaders and inhabitants did evil in the sight of the true God. Consequently, contemporary leaders who want to build enduring transformative organizations must develop themselves, their followers, and their successors to know, obey, and follow the true God and avoid His wrath. They must understand that righteous spiritual formation is important in leadership development, succession planning, and management and that physical competencies are not enough. Let us now look at the physical and emotional health component of the personal leadership poverty framework.

Leadership and physical/ emotional health

Good physical health is of great importance to leaders, as they require physical strength and stamina to carry out the tasks of leadership. The Bible teaches us that "if anyone will not work, neither shall he eat" (2 Thess. 3:10 NKJV), indicating that work is essential for purposeful living. However, all work and no rest can lead to physical and emotional breakdown. The Bible informs us that after creating the earth and man, God "rested on the seventh day from all His work which He had done" (Gen. 2:2). K. Unglaub argues that this work/rest action by God demonstrates the proper sequence for healthy living—that work precedes rest; that work without rest, or rest without work, are antithetical to the design of humans. He asserts that physical and mental activities require/expend energy and create wastes. As our energy levels go down and wastes accumulate, fatigue sets in and rest becomes desirable. Fatigue is in fact protective as it makes us aware of our need to rest. While physical activities relax the muscles, prolonged mental activities tense the muscles. Hence, a combination of physical and mental activities enhances rest.[5] During rest and sleep, the body replaces tissue cells, energy is restored, and wastes are eliminated. Also, vital organs like the heart rest as they relatively slow down. Given the triune nature of man—body, soul, and spirit—it is important that we practice physical, mental/emotional, and spiritual rest. Spiritual rest entails resting in the Lord, putting our faith in Him, fasting, praying, thanksgiving, and praising and worshipping Him.

When we don't rest, burnout can set in. According to D. Cassandra, burnout emanates from disconnects between our values, capabilities, aspirations, and work realities. Consequently, a well-motivated worker in a certain job may suffer burnout when dynamic work or organizational changes create discontinuities that lead to disconnections between his values, capabilities, aspirations and those of his new job/position requirements.[6] Reichel and Neumann describe burnout as a state of physical, emotional, and mental exhaustion, as well as cynicism toward one's work in response to chronic organizational and/or personal stressors.[7]

Organizational stressors include dynamic environmental, socio-economic, and leadership changes, and internal politics. Personal indulgencies—drugs/alcohol, smoking, immorality, lack of exercise, and so on—are also key contributors to burnout. The physical symptoms of burnout include lateness to work, feeling weak, run-down or tired, exhibition of low energy and fatigue. The emotional symptoms include lack of trust of the organization and lack of concern or interest on the job. The mental symptoms include feeling depressed, worthless, hopeless, disillusioned and rejected.

One prophet of God who exhibited symptoms of burnout in the Bible was Elijah. He aspired to eliminate the worship of Baal from Israel. After the battle on Mount Carmel (a great work), he thought that the task was over. However, Jezebel's threat changed his work realities. Consequently, he experienced burnout (frustration that he would not meet his aspirations) and ran away (1 Kings 18 and 19). If he had rested, reflected on the tasks yet to be accomplished, and consulted God on the challenge, he might not have suffered burnout. Also, owing to poor/uncontrolled emotions (emotional poverty), Saul several times tried to pin David to the wall while he was serving in his house (1 Sam. 18:11). He even attempted on one occasion to kill his son Jonathan (1 Sam. 20:33). Moreover, Rehoboam, Solomon's son, lost his reign over Israel because of poor emotional intelligence (2 Kings 12). He was unable to correctly sense the changes in his environment and accordingly adapt. In our current globalized world, where change is rapid and unpredictable, adaptation, innovation, emotional intelligence, and good human relations have become very critical to successful leadership and organizational survival.

According to D. Goleman, emotional intelligence refers to "the capacity for recognizing our own feelings and those of others, for motivating ourselves, and for managing emotions well in ourselves and in our relationships."[8] From a systems viewpoint, emotional intelligence involves knowing/managing self and the environment (beliefs, values, intrigues, intents, and actions of persons/groups) around us. According to Goleman's taxonomy, it entails self-awareness (know thyself—strengths/weaknesses), self-management (e.g., self-control, adaptability), social awareness (understanding the good/evil socio-political constituents of our environment), and social skills (e.g., initiative, empathy, communication, bond building, and relationship management). David exhibited extreme emotional intelligence when he feigned madness in the presence of the king of Gath so that he could escape from him (1 Sam. 21:10–15). Paul also exhibited rich emotional intelligence when he tried to preach about Christ to Athenians from their inscription of the "unknown God" (Acts 17:23).

From my experience and survey of the work/life balance of some executive leaders, I found that the following helped leaders to unwind and overcome work stressors:

- good family life—decent/stable spouse, good parent/children relationships
- decent personal home—preferably mortgage-free
- sports/regular exercise
- traveling to other cities/countries and sightseeing
- reading and personal development

- social activities; outside-of-work/professional relationships
- participating in nonprofit or community-development activities

Also, according to L. Wharton,[9] leaders can contribute to reducing burnout in workplaces through:

- positive role modeling—taking requisite breaks/leave, exhibiting healthy work/life balance, non-indulgence in heavy drinking/smoking, and so on;
- effective/regular communication with staff, including having one-on-one sessions, so as to feel the pulse of employees and keep them well-informed. Doubts tend to create uncertainties and fears, which contribute to burnout;
- continuously training/developing staff to have the requisite competencies for their changing jobs.
- educating people about burnout—contributors, symptoms, how to avoid/address burnout, and so on; and
- encouraging employees to develop good external support—good family and social networks, church fellowship, and so on.

Overall, leaders who want to succeed in our complex and ever-changing global environment have to develop themselves and followers to be physically strong and rich in emotional intelligence. Let us now look at the good character, integrity, and requisite competence component of the personal leadership poverty framework.

Leadership and good character, integrity and requisite competence

Although good character/integrity and requisite competence can be separately developed by leaders, I have integrated them in this write-up because they collectively engender trust, which is essential for success in leadership. According to R. Rardin, leadership is an inside-out phenomenon. It flows from character to conduct. B. Winston asserts that leadership starts from values and is expressed in relationships. According to Winston, values are prioritized entities that we prefer or consider important. They guide our choices, decisions, judgments, and evaluations. They form the bedrock of our motives, character, and conduct. They are formed essentially through our personal experiences, education, family/peer influences, work, societal norms, regulations and practices.

Beliefs are the ways we think our values can be realized. Thus, two persons or organizations (or churches) may have the same values, but their beliefs may differ. For example, Christians and Muslims value the concept and worship of one (monotheistic) God, but their beliefs (how to realize the value) are different. Values extend beyond human relationships, while morals tend to focus on good and bad conduct or behaviors in human interactions. Ethics are codes of values, conduct, or behavioral standards that an organization, society, or nation has written and instituted to guide human actions and decisions. While values are personalized and intrinsic, ethics are extrinsic and imposed by organizations, society, or legislation like the Sarbanes Oxley Act.

From my experience, most organizational codes of ethics and legislation like the Sarbanes Oxley Act are instruments that appeal to the "heads," not the "hearts" of leaders. According to Jensen and Meckling's agency theory, they are control instruments in a world where leaders essentially act as agents who want to maximize personal benefits, like those of their shareholders. Consequently, leaders and followers continuously develop clever means to beat such instruments; hence, unethical practices continue to abound.[10] On the other hand,

Davis and associates' stewardship theory enjoins us to develop leaders to act like good stewards, who put their masters' or organizational interests above personal interests; that is, leaders who want to serve, rather than just benefit.[11] The challenge for organizational leaders is how to change or renew people's hearts to become good stewards and not mere agents.

The Bible teaches us that God looks mainly at the state of the heart in choosing leaders. He chose David in preference to his senior brothers because of the state of his heart (1 Sam. 16:7). He also rejected Solomon as a leader when his heart was turned away from Him by pagan women (1 Kings 11:9). Two key attributes that the Lord looks for in the hearts of leaders are humility and the fear of God. Humility (power under control) enables the leader to serve and be teachable in varying circumstances, while the fear of God makes him obey His commandments and exhibit integrity that enables building of trust in relationships.

According to B. Winston, leadership is relationship, and trust is the basis of all good and lasting relationships. S.R. Covey stated that trust (or lack of it) is at the root of leadership and organizational success or failure. Trust engenders confidence and commitment, while distrust creates fear, suspicion, and apathy that de-motivate and destroy organizations. Covey opined that trustworthiness is based on leader character and competence.[12] B. Kellerman also attributed bad leadership to unethical practices (bad character) and ineffectiveness (incompetence).[13] Covey and Merrill asserted that character includes integrity, motive, and intent, while competency includes capability, skills, results, and track record.[14] From a biblical perspective and Winston's assertion, one would add benevolence or the state of the heart of leaders toward followers (love for others vs. love for self), which may be subsumed under character, as a major contributor to trustworthiness and trust building. Overall, the three key factors that contribute to personal trustworthiness are:

- **Integrity**—when values-in-use and actions are aligned with espoused values and prior agreements. In other words, when our yes is yes and our no is no.
- **Competence**—having the requisite knowledge, experience, skills, and attitude to carry out an assigned task.
- **Benevolence**—caring for others and having a positive motive towards others while relating with them.

Followers want to trust their leaders. Without trust, it is difficult to get followership commitment, which is essential in building transformative organizations. We will now look at the human relationship component of the personal leadership framework.

Leadership and human relationships

According to Winston and Patterson, leadership is relationship, as it essentially entails human interactions that are directed toward achieving a collective purpose and getting results.[15] According to Blanchard and associates, good relationships and good results reflect good leadership.[16] As discussed above, trustworthiness is central to building lasting relationships (and subsequently getting results), and it is the "self"—values, character and competence—that the leader brings to the leadership relationship that determines his success. Leadership relationships progress from one-on-one to team/family and subsequently to organization/community. To be effective, leaders must develop themselves to be successful at all these different levels of human interactions. According to Blanchard and associates' situational leadership model, leaders have to match their leadership or relationship style to the development levels of their constituents—"different styles for different folks." They categorized the maturity of followers into four stages:

- D1—low competence/high motivation (essentially new joiners who are eager to learn but have limited skills).
- D2—some competence/low motivation (essentially persons with experience whose motivation has waned over time).
- D3—high competence/variable motivation (essentially persons with sound knowledge/experience but have motivational challenges).
- D4—high competence/high motivation (those that are firing on four cylinders).

They opined that leaders have to employ different leadership styles—telling/directing, coaching, participating, and delegating—to match the different leadership situations. D. Goleman also provided six different leadership styles—namely visionary, coaching, affiliative, democratic, pacesetting, and commanding—that leaders can utilize (or occasionally switch to) depending on the emotional situation they face and the climate they wish to create.[17] Irrespective of the situation and leadership styles, B. Winston asserts that leaders must display "agapao love"—righteous love that is rooted in high moral standards and entails doing the right things in the right manner and with the right method for the good of all. Overall, leaders who want to build transformative organizations have to develop themselves and followers to be rich in good human relations. We will now look at the physical/spiritual security component of the personal leadership poverty framework.

Leadership and physical/spiritual security

Our Lord Jesus Christ taught us that there are two forces or powers at play in the world. There is an evil force or power, which He described as the "thief" that comes to steal, kill, and destroy; while there is also a positive force, which He represents, that gives life and life more abundantly (John 10:10 NKJV). Also, the Bible teaches that in the last days, perilous times will come and

> men will be lovers of themselves, lovers of money, boasters, proud, blasphemers, disobedient to parents, unthankful, unholy, unloving, unforgiving, slanderers, without

self-control, brutal, despisers of good, traitors, headstrong, haughty, lovers of pleasure rather than lovers of God. (2 Tim. 3: 2-4 NKJV)

In a nutshell, evil, unwholesome behavior and lawlessness will abound (and grow), while the love of many will grow cold (Matt. 24:12). I believe we are living in such a world at this time, where there is strong competition and conflict between good and evil, and consequently, much insecurity. Interestingly, the issue of insecurity has physical and spiritual dimensions.

A review of the Bible shows that successful leaders were able to fight and win physical and spiritual battles/wars. The key to their success was righteous alignment with the true God, to whom belongs power, might, strength, riches, victory and honor (1 Chron. 29:11-12). For example, David defeated Goliath with spiritual help from God. Also, through personal/collective fasting, praying, praising and worshipping the true God (2 Chron. 20), Jehoshaphat successfully overcame the Moabites, Ammonites and others that rose up against him. Moreover, Nehemiah, Mordecai and Esther successfully defeated their enemies through the help of God.

To be able to contain the negative impact of the spread of evil and unrighteousness around the world, contemporary leaders must develop themselves and their followers to be able to fight and win physical and in particular spiritual battles/wars. This requires the development of the requisite knowledge/competencies and alignment with the true God. Complacency exposes leaders, their families and their constituents to the vagaries of evil, and this is poor leadership security. We will now look at the financial stewardship component of the personal leadership poverty framework.

Leadership and financial stewardship

Several companies have collapsed because of the poor financial stewardship of their leaders. A review of the actions of the leaders of these failed organizations showed that they were greedy and self-centered. Essentially they acted as agents (hirelings), not stewards. The Bible teaches us that "he who is greedy for gain troubles his own house, but he who hates bribes will live" (Prov. 15:27 NKJV). We learn from this Scripture that greedy leaders create troubles for their organizations. They are like hirelings (agents) who flee (take care of only themselves) when they face challenges (see the wolf coming) because they do not care about the sheep (their followers and organization) (Matt. 10:11–13). Jesus also taught us in the parables of talents and the shrewd servant (Matt. 25 and Luke 16) that good financial stewardship pays; that we have to be good with little as well as with much, for "he who is unjust in least is also unjust in much" (Luke 16:10b) and "if you have not been faithful in what is another man's, who will give you your own?" (Luke 16:12). In general, good financial stewardship is critical to leadership success.

Overall, assessing and developing leaders to overcome the personal leadership poverty states elaborated above enables the building of transformative and enduring global organizations.

Chapter 3

The Leader as Light: A Concept for Developing Global Leaders

We live in a world where no nation or group of people is self-sufficient in natural resources or the factors of production. Consequently, nations and peoples of the world are interdependent. Technological advancements; improvements in trade, transportation, communication, financial services, and education; global treaties and several other factors have contributed to making the world an interdependent "global village." Currently, every organization, whether it remains at home or moves overseas, will have to become competitive in global terms in order to consistently thrive. Those that consider themselves "domestic" have to evolve and implement strategies to deal with the impact of global changes (technology, market preferences, production costs, regulations etc.) on their organizations, while those that decide to go overseas must develop the requisite capabilities to do so. Hence, developing global leaders has become a strategic imperative for most organizations. Unfortunately, several current leaders appear "blinded" and controlled by their native cultures, individual preferences and limited experiences, which prevent them from being global leaders. How can organizations develop leaders to be open (remove cross-cultural barriers) and able to see from the perspectives of other peoples and nations, so that all can thrive in a globalized world?

We will start by looking at the key characteristics and requirements of global leadership. Then I shall elaborate on the concept of the global "leader as light" and subsequently provide tips for becoming a successful global leader.

Characteristics and requirements of global leaders

According to W. Hitt, the only true perspective that enhances global leadership is the perspective of flourishing humans across the world [1]. He described as evil and antithetic to global leadership development, a contrary perspective that thwarts human flourishing through selfish conquest of one group by another. Hitt's assertion corroborates the statement of our Lord Jesus Christ that "I have come that they may have life, and that they may have it more abundantly" (John 10:10b). Consequently, I would describe leaders who go into other countries only to take home economic benefits as thieves "who have come to steal, kill and destroy" (John 10:10a). They are not global leaders. Global leaders should have the mind-set of promoting flourishing humans across the globe.

According to Rosen and associates [2] and Black and associates [3], some of the key requirements to becoming a global leader include:

- contribution—making a difference and contributing to societal development in other nations;
- good communication—engaging in genuine dialogue and taking inputs from "locals" in global decisions;
- compassion— actively caring for the well-being of others;
- cooperation and collaboration—working with others to achieve a common goal;
- ability to hold conflicting thoughts and facts at the same time; ability to manage and live with paradox, ambiguity, and perplexities;

- ability to act globally and locally at the same time—balancing "going native" and "being global"—which requires a deep understanding of local and global views;
- good knowledge of history, geography, economics, politics/government, law/judicial systems, religion/spirituality and psychology;
- ability to frame/reframe issues and view them from diverse perspectives;
- ability to emotionally connect with others and build collaborative relationships;
- ability to earn trust and be seen as transparent;
- ability to transform conflicts into creative actions; and
- being humble and able to continuously learn, and manage learning anxieties—the distress and uncertainty of personal ignorance.

According to Heifetz and associates [4], global leaders encounter more adaptive than technical challenges; hence, they have to be more adaptive than technical. Technical challenges are those with known solutions that can be embedded in work processes and procedures. Leaders only need to learn and appropriately apply the requisite solutions when faced with technical challenges. Adaptive challenges have no known unique solutions. Leaders need to adapt and mobilize their constituents to change their attitudes, thought processes, relationship styles, work habits and so on, to understand and address such challenges.

According to Marquardt and Berger,[5] some key differences in the leadership competencies required to address technical versus adaptive/global challenges are:

- Technical leaders take charge and provide decisive leadership, while adaptive/global leaders act as facilitators, allowing leadership to emerge. For example, technical leaders tend to come up with the vision and mobilize people to follow their vision. Adaptive/global leaders facilitate emergence of a collective vision that drives sometimes independent and autonomous teams to act.
- Technical leaders tend to build hierarchical organizations, while adaptive/global leaders encourage building network organizations with trusting relationships.
- Technical leaders define the problem and provide solutions, while adaptive/global leaders facilitate inquiry using probing questions and building alternative scenarios.

- Technical leaders promote linear thinking, where the past is used to predict the future. Adaptive/global leaders promote systems thinking, whereby the whole is analyzed, weaknesses are addressed, and strengths are used to harness opportunities.
- Technical leaders maintain norms, while adaptive/global leaders challenge unproductive norms.

Differentiating between international and global leadership

It is pertinent to highlight that there is a fine difference between the international leader and the global leader. The international leader grapples with inter-country issues and tends to want to "impose" the values, practices and culture of the head office—"the superior culture"—on the organizations in other countries. This can lead to conflict of cultures; hence, the international leader tends to hone his conflict-resolution and negotiating skills. On the other hand, the global leader is like the apostle Paul, who was willing to "become all things to all men, that I might by all means save some" (1 Cor. 9:22). The global leader has no singular "home-office" culture that he "trades" with other nations. He is humble enough to accept some degree of "deculturation" as he blends the various layers of culture to create a new culture that enables all to thrive and realize the organization's global strategic vision.

Given the uncertainties, perplexities, and adaptations that global leaders handle, Marquardt and Berger argue that they have to be servant leaders. Some of the fundamental characteristics of servant leaders include effective listening, empathy, healing broken spirits, awareness of self and others, good stewardship of resources, commitment to the growth of others, and community building. Becoming a global leader entails personal transformation, a transformation from singularity to plurality and multiple perspectives; from self/internal focus to other focus and boundarylessness; from "I know it all" to "I need to humble myself and continuously learn"; from love of one's country and people to love of other nations and peoples; from cultural "blindness" to cultural "light/insight" and having thoughts of peace and not of evil toward others (people, nations, organizations, etc.) "to give you a future and a hope" (Jer. 29:11 NKJV). Overall, I would argue that becoming a successful global leader entails becoming "the light of the world" that Jesus enjoined His followers to be as they "go into all the world and preach the gospel to every creature" (Mark 16:15 NKJV).

The concept of the leader as light

The Bible teaches us that the almighty God who is the overall leader of the universe (the supreme global leader) is Light (1 John 1:5), and Jesus told us that He wants us to be global leaders (Mark 16:15). Consequently, I assert that if we can emulate and practice some of His attributes as Light, we will become successful global leaders. Given that God is divine and invisible, I would argue that the light of God is different from and more encompassing than physical light. However, knowledge of the characteristics of physical light will give us insight into some of the characteristics of the Light of God and key attributes that we need to develop to be successful global leaders ("the light of the world").

Understanding the nature of light

Light is energy, and physicists refer to all forms of electromagnetic waves as light. There are essentially two broad categories of physical light—visible and invisible light. Visible light is what we see with the naked eyes. It is not really the light that we see, but the colors that are reflected by the objects that light falls on that we see. There are other forms of light, such as gamma rays, X-rays, ultraviolet light, infrared light and microwaves, which we do not see. They are invisible and can only be detected by special instruments or their manifestations when they impact on objects. Some of the uses of physical light (invisible and visible) include internal imaging, bag checking (X-ray), healing (infrared), heating/cooking (microwave), improvement of visibility (white light), remote sensing/control (infrared), checking counterfeit currency (UV), and photography.

Every light has a source. Physical light comes from physical sources, for example, matchsticks, candle wax, batteries, electricity/electric bulbs, and so on. The light from God, which is divine light, is eternal and invisible. A basic difference between divine light and physical light is that divine light has wisdom and intelligence; it can sense its environment, it is creative, and it gives life (John 1:3–4). The Bible teaches us that an analogue to divine light is the sun; hence, it states that the "Lord God is our sun" (Ps. 84:11 NLT). The sun symbolizes purity. It sustains life. Without it, most plants and even humans will die. It is enduring and stable in the midst of storms and perturbations.

It cannot be attacked, overpowered, or taken by assault. It separates day (symbolizing good) from night (symbolizing darkness and bad). We can infer from these attributes of light, some of the key requirements for becoming successful global leaders ("the light of the world"). Global leaders as "the light of the world" must:

1. Be visionary and creative.
2. Sustain life and contribute to flourishing humanity.
3. See/understand different perspectives, shades of opinions, and cultures.
4. Check and understand the "internals" of people—their values, desires, drivers, experiences, failures, and successes—in order to rightfully connect with them and employ the right persons for the right job.
5. Exhibit purity—righteousness, justice, equity, and high moral standards.
6. Be able to thrive in the midst of storms and environmental changes.
7. Protect themselves, organizational resources and constituents from hostile attacks.
8. Weed out evil thoughts and practices (for example, occultism, harm to people and environment etc.) that offend their source of light—the God of the universe.

A key question is "How do organizations develop people to become 'the light of the world' and successful global leaders?"

Becoming a global leader—the light of the world

The Bible teaches us that "the entrance of Your words gives light; it gives understanding to the simple" (Ps. 119:130 NKJV). Hence, I would argue that becoming "the light of the world" entails imbibing and living by the Word of God in the Bible. When we live by the word of God, the word becomes "a lamp to our feet and a light to our path" in our global leadership journey (Ps. 119:105 NKJV). Based on the Beatitudes taught by Jesus (Matt. 5:1–11), B. Winston [6] argues that when leaders truly imbibe the word of God, they:

1. Become poor in spirit, humble and teachable.
2. Mourn and care for others as our Lord is a caring Father.
3. Exhibit controlled discipline and become harmless to others.
4. Become righteous, morally upright and ethical in thoughts and actions.
5. Become merciful and forgiving.

6. Become peacemakers, not just peaceful. They tend to develop ability to manage and transform conflicts for mutual benefits and improved relationships.
7. Are able to withstand and outlast persecutions.
8. Exhibit moral love and become truly successful global leaders—"the light of the world."

Chapter 4

Leadership Theories and Practices

Therefore give to Your servant an understanding heart to judge Your people, that I may discern between good and evil. For who is able to judge this great people of Yours?
—1 Kings 3:9 NKJV

He sought God in the days of Zechariah, who had understanding in the visions of God; and as long as he sought the LORD, God made him prosper.
—2 Chronicles 26:5 NKJV

Knowledge is the accumulation of facts and information; understanding is having insight into how/why things work or occur; wisdom is the application of knowledge and understanding.

Theories attempt to explain or enable understanding of observed events, occurrences, activities, happenings, or phenomena. They provide understanding about how and why certain occurrences take place. The development of theories usually starts from observations, followed by hypotheses (proposed theories), testing, analyses of test results, proof of reliability (repeatability) and validity (correctness), and the conditions under which reliability and validity occur. Given the relative stability of physical, chemical and biological systems in nature, the concepts of reliability (repeatability), validity (correctness) and the conditions under which they occur are key requirements in the acceptance of scientific theories. However, in leadership studies, where we are dealing with humans (leaders, followers, and constituents) who are multifaceted and can change or even reverse themselves under the same conditions, several theories are usually required to understand an observed phenomenon, and it is very important to know the situations, conditions, constraints, or otherwise under which a proposed theory is applicable. Theories (especially tested/proven ones) enhance practice, while results from practice also provide inputs into the development of theories. A knowledge of leadership theories and their applicability (where, when and how they are applicable) will enhance your understanding and practice of leadership. Let us now review some leadership theories.

The great man theory

This theory hypothesizes that leaders are great persons, who are born, not made. It emanated from a heroic and militaristic view of leaders as people who lead their followers (nations/groups/organizations) to war and win. It has a conquest, aristocratic (rule of the best, who are privileged by birth or wealth), and male-dominated view of leadership. Although there is some element of "greatness" in leadership, the world defines "greatness" in a different way from the Bible. Our Lord Jesus said,

> You know that the rulers of the Gentiles lord it over them, and those who are great exercise authority over them. Yet, it shall not be so among you; but whoever desires to become great among you, let him be your servant. And whoever desires to be first among you, let him be your slave, just as the Son of Man did not come to be served, but to serve and give His life a ransom for many. (Matt. 20:25-28 NKJV)

We learn from this Scripture that greatness is in service of God and man, not in overpowering others or making them to look powerless. Our God is great in the attributes that characterize Him; He is great in His acts and the outcomes of His acts. He uses His greatness to do awesome things for the good of mankind. Our God is great all round. Some specific aspects of His greatness include:

- holiness
- strength, power, and ability
- size
- justice and righteousness
- love, mercy, and forgiveness
- knowledge, understanding, and wisdom
- creativity, achievements, and victories
- working miracles
- wealth
- faithfulness
- humility
- punishing the wicked and unrepentant

(Some key reference Scriptures are 1 Chron. 29:10–13, Ps. 62:11, Ps. 104, Ps. 145, and John 3:16.)

God has given each and everyone some degree of "greatness" to serve Him and mankind. Hence, leadership is not limited to "great men," as proposed by the great man theory. It is to the degree that we develop and use our God-given talents to serve

God and man that we become "great leaders" in our areas of calling and service.

Trait theory

Traits are habitual predispositions or patterns of thoughts, emotions and behaviors. They differ across individuals and can be relatively stable; hence, they are often used to classify personalities. When the great man theory was unable to fully explain the leadership phenomenon, some researchers turned to traits. They studied the traits of successful leaders and hypothesized that people with the traits of successful leaders can be developed to also become successful leaders.

R. M. Stogdill identified some of the following traits and skills (which are different from traits) as critical to leadership success [1]:

Traits	Skills
• ambitious and achievement oriented	• fluent in speaking
• cooperative	• knowledge of task
• decisive	• organized
• persistent	• working with others
• energetic	• persuasive
• dependable	

| • alert to environmental changes | |

McCall and Lombardo identified four primary traits that could make leaders succeed or fail/derail if they are absent [2]:

- emotional stability and composure—being calm, confident and largely predictable even when under stress
- admitting error—owning mistakes rather than digging in to cover them up
- good interpersonal capability—able to communicate and persuade others without resort to negative or coercive tactics
- intellectual breadth—able to understand a wide range of areas, rather than have a narrow area of expertise or be narrow-minded

A key challenge with trait theories is that different traits and capabilities are required for different leadership situations. What worked in one situation may be unsuitable for another. Hence, researchers started moving to behavioral and situational theories to explain leadership phenomena.

Behavioral theory

Behavior is the response of a system or organism to various stimuli or inputs, which may be internal or external, covert or overt, voluntary or involuntary. Behaviors can be innate (ingrained by nature) or learned (nurtured). In general, learning or nurturing can control or moderate innate tendencies. Hence, according to the behavioral theory of leadership, leadership can be learned (nurtured); leaders can be made, they are not born.

Behavioral theories assume that successful leadership can be defined in the discernable actions that leaders take. These actions can be learned; they need not depend on or be related to traits that have to be measured through psychometric tests. Observing and documenting the actions or inactions of successful and failed leaders is the basis of the behavioral theory of leadership. Research conducted by Kouzes and Posner indicated five behavioral practices that enable leaders to get extraordinary things done [3]. These are:

- **Modeling the Way**
  Successful leaders lead by example. Their deeds are consistent with their words. Their actions portray their real values.

They promote consistent progress and build commitment through being trustworthy.

- **Inspiring a Shared Vision**
  Successful leaders inspire or drive the envisioning of an uplifting and ennobling future. They enlist others in a common vision through connection of values, interests, hopes and desires.

- **Challenging the Process**
  Successful leaders challenge existing processes and practices. They drive creativity, innovation, continuous improvement and growth. They experiment, take risks and learn from mistakes. They continuously search their environment for new opportunities.

- **Enabling Others to Act**
  Successful leaders empower others by developing them and providing tools, resources, authority and decision rights that enable them to act. They promote collaborative work environments, where people freely share knowledge and support each other to improve collective performance.

- **Encouraging the Heart**
  Successful leaders celebrate team accomplishments and recognize individual contributions to achievement of team goals.

Overall, behavioral theories postulate that successful leadership is based on definable, learnable behaviors. In fact, the personal leadership poverty model, which I developed, can be classified as a behavioral theory.

Situational leadership theory

Ken Blanchard is the key proponent of situational leadership. As was highlighted in Chapter 2, he observed that leaders exhibit both supportive and directive behaviors, and that successful leaders assess the capability levels of their constituents and accordingly align their leadership styles. According to Blanchard and associates [4], leaders have to match their leadership or relationship style to the development levels of their constituents—"different styles for different folks." They categorized the maturity of followers into four stages, namely:

- D1—low competence/high motivation or commitment (essentially new joiners who are eager to learn but have limited skills).

- D2—some competence/low motivation or commitment (essentially persons with experience whose motivation has waned over time).
- D3—high competence/variable motivation or commitment (essentially persons with sound knowledge/experience but have motivational challenges).
- D4—high competence/high motivation (those that are firing on four cylinders).

Blanchard and associates asserted that leaders have to employ different (supporting or directing) leadership styles to match the different followership competency and commitment situations. The four leadership styles are:

> *telling/directing,* which is appropriate for D1.
> *coaching* is appropriate for D2.
> *supporting/participating* is appropriate for D3.
> *delegating* is appropriate for D4.

Telling

The telling leader defines the roles and tasks for each follower and then supervises the followers very closely. All important decisions are made by the leader and communicated essentially one-way to the followers. This may be appropriate for new workers who are motivated but have limited or low competencies.

Coaching/Selling

The coaching/selling leader works with followers to define the roles and tasks of the followers. The leader strives to motivate and build up the followers so that they can further develop/motivate themselves to accomplish set goals. Communication is two-way.

Supporting/Participating

The supporting or participating leader focuses on motivating his or her followers (who are generally experienced/competent but with variable motivation) to succeed. He or she provides the requisite resources and emphasizes the business case, the rewards/recognition and the consequences for success or failure. He or she partakes in decision making to get followership commitments and leaves implementation to followers.

Delegating

The leader delegates but retains his or her ultimate accountability. Hence, he or she monitors, uses external auditors to ensure compliance and accordingly drives continuous improvements.

D. Goleman, from his emotional leadership studies, also provided six situational leadership styles that leaders can utilize (or occasionally switch to) depending on the emotional situation they face and climate they wish to create [5]. These are:

- visionary
- coaching
- affiliative
- democratic
- pacesetting
- commanding

Visionary

Visionary leaders work with the constituents to build a shared vision. They also enable the followers to see how their work fits into the big picture, thus providing people with a clear sense that what they do matters. Trustworthiness and transparency enhance visionary leadership.

Coaching

A coaching leader communicates to his constituents (through deep personal conversations, his actions, provision of resources, development opportunities etc.) that he believes in their potentials and expects them to grow and win.

Affiliative

Affiliative leaders value people and their feelings. They place more emphasis on employees' emotional needs than on simply accomplishing tasks and goals. Their emphasis on building emotional bondage and providing emotional support to followers, especially during difficult times, enables them to build tremendous loyalty and interconnectedness, which helps in complex and difficult situations. Some Asian (Chinese, Japanese), South American, and African cultures value the affiliative leadership style. Consequently, they tend not to want to do business with those they don't feel affiliated with.

Democratic

Democratic leadership is suitable in complex and ambiguous situations, when the problems and requisite solutions are ill-defined and people are afraid of the unknown. By allowing or enabling all to participate and be part of the problem definition and solution making, the leader builds trust and earns the confidence of his or her constituents. Democratic leadership is enhanced when constituents are knowledgeable and capable. The leader hears all and allows all to participate in the decision making.

Pacesetting

Pacesetting leaders are exemplary. They usually set high performance standards for themselves and followers. This style is good if the leader is righteous and knows where he or she is going, and his or her constituents can follow. Otherwise, it can create a situation where the blind follow the blind into a ditch. Some Christian leaders who made their congregations believe that rapture would occur or Jesus would come on a certain date are examples of wrong pacesetters who have led their followers astray.

Commanding

Commanding leaders give clear instructions about tasks/missions and the direction or method to follow. This may be useful in times of emergency or crises, when people are afraid or don't know what to do. It is important that the leader himself or herself knows what to do or how to seek help; otherwise, he or she will lead himself or herself and followers into a ditch.

Overall, leaders usually have a preferred or dominant style. It is pertinent for them to know that to be successful, they need different leadership styles for different situations. Hence, they need to develop their leadership capabilities to handle diverse situations.

Contingency Theories

Contingency theories postulate that there is no one way to lead, that successful leadership is contingent (or dependent) on the prevailing factors that define the leadership setting. Consequently, leaders need to know the prevailing factors upon which leadership success is contingent and accordingly align their behaviors, styles and practices. The key factors upon which leadership success is contingent are:

- followership motivation. How you lead and get people to work is dependent on how motivated they are. It is easier to lead self-motivated than ill-motivated or depressed followers;
- followership capability with respect to task. It is easier to lead capable than incapable or partially capable persons to achieve a set goal;
- leadership assessment or perception of followers. The leader's poor assessment of a follower may affect the type of tasks he or she assigns to the follower;
- leadership affection for followers. Some leaders have more affection for some followers than others. Also, some leaders feel more comfortable working with followers from the same tribe, race, culture, or religion;
- leadership power. The position of the leader and his or her personal powers play key roles in what the leader can accomplish;
- complexity of the task. Accomplishing complex tasks most times requires cross-functional efforts. Integration of key activities is therefore central to leadership success;

- complexity of the environment. Some external environments provide more support and consequently are more congenial for achieving certain kinds of work;
- organizational complexity. Leaders require complex networking and consultations in complex organizations before they achieve tasks; and
- reward or loss (punishment) attached to accomplishing task or achieving the set goals.

Whereas situational leadership focuses more on the follower's situation, that is, given the follower's situation, what should the leader do—apply directive or supporting styles?, contingency theories take into account the leadership capability and other organizational/environmental factors (not just followership) that affect leadership success.

In F. E. Fieldler's contingency theory, leadership styles are defined as task-oriented or relationship-oriented [6]. The contingent factors are:

- leader-follower relations. The degree of confidence, loyalty and attraction that followers/leaders have toward each other

affect their interactions and leadership success;
- task structure. Tasks that are clear and structured, with clear process/procedures/standards and delivery times, provide enhanced leader control, followership development and assessment. Unstructured tasks require flexibility and a higher degree of freedom in leader/followership interactions; and
- position power. The leader's position power is high or low depending on his or her ability to reward or "punish" followers.

Overall, we learn from Fieldler's theory that the leadership styles (task- or relationship-oriented) and contingent factors (leader/follower relations, task structure and power positions) have to be considered in the selection, development and matching of leaders/followers in order to achieve organization goals.

Path-Goal theory

This theory postulates that leadership success is based on the achievement of paths, goals and how leaders motivate their followers to achieve set paths/goals. Leaders who focus on paths and goals define clear goals, clarify path(s) to the goals, remove obstacles and provide resources/support to followers/constituents to achieve set goals.

Exemplary is the leadership of the Redeemed Christian Church of God (RCCG), which follows the path-goal theory in its drive to achieve its mission/vision.

The RCCG path/goals are:

1. To make heaven.
2. To take as many people as possible.
3. To have a member of the Redeemed Christian Church of God in every family of all nations.
4. To accomplish number one above, holiness will be our lifestyle.
5. To accomplish numbers two and three above, we will plant churches within five minutes' walking distance in every city and town of developing countries and within five minutes' driving distance in every city and town of developed countries.
6. We will pursue these objectives until every nation in the world is reached for Jesus Christ, our Lord!

Leader-Member exchange (LMX) theory

This theory postulates that the process and quality of leader-member(s) interactions is pivotal to leadership success. The key contributory factors to effective leader-member(s) interactions are: trust, honesty, loyalty, good communications, clarity of roles/responsibilities, commitment to continuous learning even from failures, commitment to a shared vision/mission, and a calling other than money or mundane benefits. Overall, a strong bond between leaders and followers enhances leadership success.

It has, however, been observed that there may be different degrees of bonding between a leader and members of a team or group, which leads to the development of inner groups (inner caucus or kitchen cabinet) and outer groups. The leader has to watch that the development of these groups does not lead to acrimony among team members. Our Lord Jesus Christ had Peter, James and John as inner-group members, but He never failed to rebuke them among the other disciples when they were wrong, indicating that being members of His inner group did not exonerate them from abiding by His values and principles.

Transactional leadership

Transactional leadership involves motivating and directing followers primarily through appealing to their own self-interest. It is based on a prior agreement or contract between the leader and follower that a certain transaction will take place after a task is accomplished. There is little or no empathy or relationship (outside the transaction) between the leader and the follower. The transactional leader believes that leadership is contingent on rewards, punishment, and the exercise of authority and power. This is usually a manager's approach to human interactions. The manager handles transactions through active management by exceptions (continuous monitoring, control, correction, and assurance of compliance with standards) or passive management by exception (monitoring and only responding to deviations from standards).

Transactional leadership can be appropriate in ensuring operational excellence, especially when the task is routine, the environment is stable and there is need to eliminate unnecessary delays and wastages. It can, however, lead to bureaucratic leadership, whereby the leader simply emphasizes compliance with processes, procedures and standards, which may themselves be old or inappropriate, and makes the organization to be noncreative and unresponsive to changes.

Laissez-faire leadership

Laissez-faire leaders tend to abdicate responsibilities and avoid making decisions. They leave their followers to be on their own, like a flock of sheep without a shepherd. The followers therefore roam about because of lack of goals and direction. Laissez-faire leadership is essentially non-transactional.

Laissez-faire leadership may be appropriate in ambiguous exploratory situations, where basic formation of ideas, concepts and research are required to define or frame problems and chart possible solution paths. In such cases, the leader simply provides an environment for experts to collaboratively interact and work on the subject matter.

It is pertinent to highlight that sin (especially idol worship and immorality) can make God become like a laissez-faire leader toward humans. The Bible teaches us that:

> Behold, the Lord's hand is not shortened that it cannot save; nor His ear heavy that it cannot hear. But your iniquities have separated you from your God; and your sins have hidden His face from you, so that He will not hear. (Isa. 59:1–2 NKJV)

Transformational leadership

> And do not be conformed to this world but be transformed by the renewing of your mind, that you may prove what is that good and acceptable and perfect will of God.
> —Romans 12:2 NKJV

In general, humans bring values, beliefs, perceptions, attitudes, knowledge, and capability, which have been shaped or formed by several factors, including their culture, education, prior experiences, and religion, to leadership situations. Moving to new levels of consciousness, capability, and performance requires leaders and followers to intrinsically, extrinsically and collectively change and move from where they are, which is transformation. According to Bass and Avolio [7], transformational leadership is portrayed when leaders:

- promote and live by higher moral and ethical standards;
- develop themselves and their constituents to higher levels of capability and potential;
- motivate their colleagues and followers to look beyond self-interest to group and societal interests. They promote the "greater good";
- promote creativity, innovation, and constructive destruction of the old; and
- drive the envisioning of new exciting futures for their organizations and constituents.

Again, according to Bass and Avolio, the key elements of transformational leadership are:

1. **Idealized or charismatic influence**
   Transformational leaders are role models to their followers. They are honest, trusted, admired, and respected. They earn their charismatic influence by selflessly caring for their followers and others and demonstrating high moral and ethical standards.

2. **Inspirational motivation**
   Transformational leaders inspire and communicate a shared bright future for all.

They motivate their followers to strive to attain the bright future.

3. **Intellectual stimulation**

   Transformational leaders stimulate and drive creativity/innovation. They promote and cherish individual and collective efforts to continuously improve. They act with a mantra that "the best is yet to come; if others can do it, we can do more." They stimulate intellectualism through the use of appropriate questions, framing and reframing issues/problems, encouraging research, experimentation, and so on.

4. **Individualized consideration**

   Transformational leaders listen to individual needs of followers and act as coaches and mentors that help their followers to become self-actualized and fulfilled.

The four "I"s of transformational leadership are enhanced by the leader acting as a steward rather than an agent (or hireling).

Agency theory

According to Jensen and Meckling [8], agency theory explains the unethical actions of leaders of a firm, who as agents, exhibit interests that are divergent from those of their principals (shareholders). According to agency theory, both parties (agents and principals) act to maximize their respective utilities. Consequently, they can develop divergent interests that are detrimental to the firm. In order to exercise control on their agents, principals usually employ audits and other corporate control and governance mechanisms. However, there have been cases where audit firms have been duplicitous, and records provided by management and audit firms did not reflect a true account of the state of a firm.

This indicates that regulations and controls external to leaders and workers may not solve the unethical practices that are plaguing many organizations. The Bible refers to leaders who act like agents as hirelings. It teaches that:

> But a hireling, he who is not the shepherd, one who does not own the sheep, sees the wolf coming and leaves the sheep and flees; and the

wolf catches the sheep and scatters them. The hireling flees because he is a hireling and does not care about the sheep. (John 10:12–13)

Stewardship theory

An alternative solution is to select and develop trustworthy leaders and workers who act as good stewards, who place the interests of their organizations above self-interests. According to Davis and associates, stewardship theory defines situations in which leaders are not motivated by individual goals, but rather are stewards whose motives are aligned with the objectives of their principals [9]. Overall, leaders who want to build enduring organizations must develop their followers to be stewards. They must be good stewards with little and as well with much as their organizations grow. Our Lord Jesus taught us that "he who is unjust in least is also unjust in much" (Luke 16:10b). Also, "if you have not been faithful in what is another man's, who will give you your own?" (Luke 16: 12).

Some other key biblical leadership concepts/models are:

1. The leader as a shepherd.
2. The leader as a servant.
3. The leader as a father or mother or parent.
4. The leader as a friend.
5. The leader as a child.
6. The leader as a soldier.
7. The leader as a disciple of Christ.

I encourage readers to research the Bible/Christian and other literature, and write about these biblical leadership concepts and models.

Overall, leadership is a complex phenomenon. Most leadership theories, concepts and models give only an inkling into some aspects of leadership. I agree with B. Winston that leadership starts from values and it is expressed in relationships. It entails relating with others with moral love (doing the right things in the right way/manner at the right time) in order to achieve set purpose and goals. Trust and trustworthiness are central to building lasting relationships (and subsequently getting results), and it is the quality of the "self" (values, character, and competence) that the leader brings to the leadership relationship that determines his or her success.

Chapter 5

Power and Influence

God has spoken once, twice I have heard this: that power belongs to God.
—Psalm 62:11 NKJV

And you shall remember the Lord your God, for it is He who gives you power to get wealth.
—Deuteronomy. 8:18a NKJV

This is what the Lord says: Don't let the wise boast in their wisdom, or the powerful boast in their power, or the rich boast in their riches. But those who wish to boast should boast in this alone: that they truly know me.
—Jeremiah 9:23–24a NLT

Power is the ability to do work or cause work to be done over time. It usually entails movement or motion. In human interactions or relationships, power is the ability of a person or organization (called an agent) to cause another person or organization (called the target) to do work, carry out an activity, or behave in a certain manner.

Usually, both the agent and target have different kinds or degrees of inherent power. Thus, power is not exclusive to leaders or superiors. Followers also have some inherent power. Hence, the use or effect of power in human interactions is a relative phenomenon. When followers use their power (e.g., knowledge) to support that of leaders, the resultant effect is great, and when they restrain the leader's power, the resultant organizational effect is sub-optimal. Authority is the power vested in a position. It is therefore exclusive to that position.

Influence is the impact or the effect of the use or application of power. It can be termed good or bad (positive or negative) depending on whether it enhances or harms (or tends to diminish) the target. Negative influence moves one to behave or take actions that are contrary to God's laws/commandments, state laws, societal norms, or the objectives of a group that one belongs to. For example, harlots, robbers, drug addicts, and so on, who may have their own influencing agents or leaders, are suffering from negative influence. Positive influence occurs when one is moved to act in accordance with the will of God and positive (condition-enhancing) goals are achieved. Also, depending on the duration of the impact on the target, an influence can be termed as momentary, short-term (over a relative short duration), transitory (changing from one level or state to another), long-lasting, or permanent. For example, Jacob's bowl of red stew was a momentary or short-term influence that made Esau to give up his birthright (Gen. 25:29–33). David's harp music, which temporarily drove a distressing spirit away from Saul, was a transitory influence (1 Sam. 16:23; 18:10–11). A born-again Christian who is committed to living a Christ-like life until his death is benefiting from a long-lasting influence.

Types and sources of power

French and Raven classified power into five different types [1], as follows:

- reward power. This is the power of the agent to reward the target. The target succumbs to or complies with the agent because he or she has the power to reward the target;
- coercive power. This is the power of the agent to punish or diminish the status of the target;
- legitimate power. This is authority or power that the agent possesses by virtue of his or her position. The target complies because the target believes the position of the agent

bestows the power on him or her and the target respects the position;
- expert power. This is derived from specialized knowledge and capability. The target complies because he or she values the expertise of the agent; and
- referent or charismatic power. This comes from the trustworthiness of the agent. The target complies because he or she believes in and admires the agent.

According to B. M. Bass [2] and Gary Yukl [3], power can be classified into two groups, namely, position power or personal power.

Position power

- legitimate power
- reward power
- coercive power
- information power
- decision power
- ecological power—control over an environment or territory
- political power—derived from the votes or support of a populace

Personal power

- expert power—knowledge, capability, technological
- referent power—inherent or intrinsic to the individual in how he or she behaves and what he or she does

Influence tactics

Gary Yukl identified the following proactive influence tactics that agents usually deploy:

1. Rational persuasion. The agent uses facts and logical arguments to show to the target the feasibility and benefits of carrying out the tasks.
2. Apprising. The agent demonstrates how carrying out the tasks will benefit the target personally and advance his or her interests.
3. Inspirational appeals. The agent inspires the target by appealing to his or her values and ideals.
4. Consultation. The agent consults the target to contribute to improving the proposal or work requirement.
5. Exchange. The agent incentivizes the target to perform.

6. Collaboration. The agent provides support and resources that enable the target to perform.
7. Personal appeals. The agent uses his or her friendship with the target to seek favor or support for the request.
8. Ingratiation. The agent praises or flatters the target to carry out the request.
9. Legitimizing. The agent uses legitimate power or authority by referring to the need to comply with laws, rules, and regulations.
10. Pressure. The agent uses persistent checks, reminders, demands, threats, and so on to make the target perform.
11. Coalition. The agent seeks the aid of others to cause the target to perform.

Human reactions to use of power and influence

According to Gary Yukl and from my experience, there are essentially four ways that humans respond or react to the use of power and influence. These are:

1. **Rebellion.** This occurs when the target overtly and violently opposes the power

and influence of the agent. This can lead to breakdown of organizational functions and coherence. This usually occurs when the core values, beliefs, key interests/aspirations, and cultural artifacts of targets are adversely impacted or perceived to be adversely impacted.

2. **Resistance.** This occurs when the target covertly opposes the influence of the agent. He or she therefore does not carry out the request or required action. Usually the target elaborates the impediments to carrying out the action or explains why the action need not be undertaken; he or she delays action, attempts to use a higher authority to stop the action, or simply pretends that action is being taken whereas nothing is being done.

3. **Compliance.** The target simply does what is required. However, he or she does not cherish or believe in it. Compliance may lead to behavioral but not attitudinal or personal value changes. For complex tasks, this may induce sloppiness and increased risk of failure as unexpected occurrences are not properly observed, diagnosed, and addressed. However, it may be appropriate for routine and low-risk activities.

4. Commitment. The target agrees with the request from the agent and is self-motivated to carry it out, even if it entails some self-sacrifice. Usually this occurs when the target trusts the agent and the organization, or the request is in line with his or her personal values and aspirations.

Some of the pertinent questions leaders must ask while trying to exercise their power and influence are: Will the stimulus motivate or satisfy followers? How will it affect followership performance? What effects will it have on group/team effectiveness and cohesion? Overall, sustainable attractiveness between the leader and follower is required for followership commitment to occur. This can be obtained mainly through transformational leadership. From my experience, the utmost followership reaction that transactional leadership can evoke is compliance. Hence, leaders need to continuously develop and improve their capabilities so that they can rely more on their personal qualities than positional power.

Chapter 6

Coaching, Counseling, Mentoring, and Discipling

Can two work together unless they are agreed?
—Amos 3:3 NKJV

And the things that you have heard from me among many witnesses, commit these to faithful men who will be able to teach others also.
—2 Timothy 2:2 NKJV

Brethren, if a man is overtaken by any trespass, you who are spiritual restore such a one in the spirit of gentleness, considering yourself lest you also be tempted. Bear one another's burden and so fulfill the law of Christ.
—Galatians 6:1 NKJV

The quality of an organization is determined by the quality of its people. Hence, leadership/followership development, succession planning, and management are critical for organizational survival and growth. Apart from formal classroom training, coaching, counseling, mentoring, and discipling are some of the methods organizations can use to develop their leaders and followers. They are based essentially on collaborative, facilitative, and empathic leadership practices.

Collaborative leadership

Collaborative leadership is required in most situations where there is no formal authority and constituents have to work together to achieve a common purpose or shared vision. According to Hank Rubin [1], "a collaboration is a purposeful relationship in which all parties strategically choose to cooperate in order to accomplish a shared outcome." The key requirements for successful collaborative leadership include:

1. A good understanding of the respective interests and values of the collaborative parties. Areas of convergence are strengthened, while areas of divergence or conflict are addressed.
2. Clarification and understanding of the context, focus issues/areas, and boundaries of the collaboration.

3. Agreeing to a set of shared values and purposes for the collaboration. Agreeing to set goals.
4. Agreeing on activities to be undertaken by the respective parties.
5. Ensuring that parties have the capability and motivation to perform or rise up to their tasks.
6. Agreeing to meetings' schedules, pattern, place and communication processes.
7. Building trust and improving relationships.
8. Agreeing on decision rights and process.
9. Agreeing on grievance or conflict-resolution process.
10. Continuous reflection and improvement to achieve set goals.
11. Agreeing on how rewards and losses are shared.

Facilitative leadership

A facilitative leader helps individuals or groups to clarify or resolve issues and improve themselves and performance. Essentially, he or she guides and helps others to improve their capability and output.

Empathic Leadership

The empathic leader places himself in the shoes of his constituents in order to understand the factors that impact them and consequently improve overall performance. He does this through openness, active listening, emotional intelligence and cultural astuteness.

We will now briefly review coaching, counseling, mentoring, and discipling as leadership/followership development methods so as to know when and how best to deploy them to improve organizational performance.

Coaching

Coaching is the practice of supporting an individual or group called the client to achieve specified set goals or results. The relationship between the coach and the client is usually formal, and it is for achieving a specific task or result over a specific period or duration. The coach is usually paid for by the client or an organization that the client works for. The process can be nondirective (collaborative/facilitative and mainly question-based, with the client committing to and carrying out improvements) or directive, with the coach issuing instructions or directives. Coaching is research-based action, as the coach usually listens actively to the client, observes the client in action, and leads mainly through feedback, exercises, and role plays that enable the client to attain the set standard or achieve the specific task. The coach usually has some experience about (or understands the nuances of) the task at hand.

Counseling

Counseling is a supportive, empathic, nonjudgmental, and facilitative leadership process that enables the counseled to heal, take appropriate or corrective actions, avoid or recover from mistakes/failures, and improve performance.

Areas where counseling is usually required include relationship issues, bereavement, marital issues, stress, illness, self-image, self-esteem, suffering from abusive behaviors/actions, career development, financial management, and spiritual life. Usually it is the person who requires counseling that approaches the counselor to establish a counseling relationship.

Mentoring

According to C. R. Bell, the principal goal of mentoring is to create a "self-directed learner."[2] The main focus of mentoring is the protégé, and the mentor's main aim is to help the protégé achieve his or her self-directed goal, not to make him or her become like the mentor or "master." Thus, the protégé in mentoring has almost complete freedom of choice and action. For example, in Mark 10:17, when a rich man asked Jesus how he could inherit eternal life, Jesus mentored him by directing him to the Holy Scriptures and commandments. When he asserted that he had obeyed the commandments all his life, Jesus suggested that he sell his earthly goods so that he could perfect his drive to achieve his goal. He exercised his free choice and left the mentoring process.

Discipling

On the other hand, discipling entails making someone or a group of persons to become like a "master"; in the case of Christianity, disciples are developed to be like Jesus Christ.

When our Lord Jesus Christ told Peter and his brother Andrew to "follow Me and I will make you fishers of men" (Matt. 4:19 NKJV), he was asking them to become his disciples. After discipling them for about three years, He commissioned them by saying, "go therefore and make disciples of all nations" (Matt. 28:19 NKJV). Persons like Peter and Andrew, who decided to become disciples, abandoned all to follow and be conformed to the "master."

Let us now look at some similarities and differences between mentoring and discipling. Thereafter, I will provide some tips for effective mentoring.

Some similarities between discipling and mentoring

1. Both are learning partnerships, in which the discipler and the mentor are more skilled and experienced than the protégé. The key goal is to improve the capability of the protégé. Thus, leaders who want to employ these techniques must not be novices.
2. Both require commitment by the discipler/disciple and mentor/protégé.
3. Both require agreement of minds and good leader/follower relationships. Leadership is really about relationship. Good relationships

reflect good leadership. If there is no good relationship between the mentor/protégé and discipler/disciple, the processes will not be effective.
4. Both require a clear learning or development purpose and endgame vision. According to C. R. Bell, a clear conviction of "as a result of this learning, you will be able to ..." is essential for effective mentoring. This is also true of discipling.
5. Both entail providing feedback and encouragement to the protégé or disciple.
6. Both the mentor in mentoring and the master in discipling become key references for the protégé or disciple. For example, in Acts 22:3, Paul "boasted" that as a Pharisee he was brought up "at the feet of Gamaliel." Also, in Acts 4:13, the high priest and his colleagues knew Peter and John were uneducated and untrained men. However, when Peter and John spoke boldly before them, they marveled and "realized that they had been with Jesus."

Some differences between discipling and mentoring

1. Mentoring is usually a one-on-one activity, while discipling can be one to many.
2. In mentoring, the protégé is groomed to become a self-directed learner who may even become "greater" than the mentor. The learning partnership grows, through self-discovery by the protégé, from one of interdependence to one of independence. Usually the mentor will ask the protégé, "What do you want to become, or what is your interest?" and the mentor will guide the protégé to undertake self-directed learning to achieve his or interest. In discipleship, the master is supreme and the subject of focus. The disciple looks up to him or her and wants to be like him or her. Dependence is maintained through obeying/following similar beliefs, regulations, processes, and practices. Jesus underscored the importance of dependence in discipleship when He told His disciples, "without me you can do nothing" (John 15:5b). He also said, "I am with you always even to the end of the age" (Matt. 28:20b).

3. Disciples have an identity, a group name. The disciples of our Lord were first called Christians at Antioch (Acts 11:26). Protégés in mentoring, even from the same mentor, may not carry the same identity.
4. Discipling usually involves obedience to a set of common rules, norms, principles, and practices by both the discipler and the disciple. On the other hand, mentoring fosters freedom, which enables the protégé to build bridges to other resources. The mentor may even link the protégé with other mentors who can help him or her to further develop his or her self-interest.

Some tips for effective mentoring by leaders

1. Have a humble heart. Reduce the power distance between you and your constituents so that they feel comfortable coming to you for mentoring.
2. Build a trustworthy relationship with those who come for mentoring. Integrity, competence and benevolence are key bases of trust. So, keep people's secrets secret. Also, "study to shew thyself approved

unto God, a workman that needeth not be ashamed, rightly dividing the word of truth" (2 Tim. 2:15 KJV).
3. Be committed to supporting the protégé. Mentoring entails a lot of conversation. So be prepared, be a good listener, and be available.
4. Jointly set learning and proficiency goals with the protégé. Encourage him or her to extend his or her learning and undertake things that will improve his or her capability and performance.
5. Give honest positive feedback. Also, encourage the protégé to seek feedback concerning his or her performance and improvement from other colleagues.
6. Be open to learning from new ideas and concepts/suggestions that the protégé may throw at you.

Chapter 7

Organizational Theories and Practices

It is difficult to solve complex problems, serve large numbers of customers, or develop societies without organizations, where people with diverse capabilities work to achieve common organizational purposes. Consequently, leaders need good insight into organizational theories and practices in order to properly lead and improve their organizations.

Organizations are deliberate human creations. People may have similar values, for example, football or music fans, vegetarians, and so on, but they do not constitute organizations unless they collectively agree to pursue a set purpose and are obligated to certain roles/responsibilities/accountabilities, systems and processes.

According to G. Morgan, metaphors and related theories help us to understand the complexities of organizations [1]. Some of the key metaphors that

Morgan uses to describe organizations and some of the related theories are:

1. Organizations as machines—the mechanistic view of organizations. Some related theories are Taylor's scientific management, Weber's theory of bureaucracy, and Fayol's administrative theory.
2. Organizations as organisms—the organismic view that sees organizations as living social entities that have social/psychological needs and can adapt to survive and thrive. General systems theory, resource dependency theory, and contingency and motivation theories are pertinent.
3. Organizations as brains—the learning organization viewpoint. Argyris's single/double loop learning, Senge's learning organization, and Leavitt/March's experience curve are pertinent.
4. Organizations as cultures—the values/beliefs/ideologies-based view of organizations. Weick's enactment theory and Schein's theory are relevant.
5. Organizations as political systems—the power/coalition/conflict view of organizations. Decision theories and strategic contingency theories are applicable.

In general, organizations are made up of "hard" parts (equipment, material/financial resources, structures, etc.) and "soft" parts (values, beliefs, vision/mission/purpose, formal/informal processes, etc.). Leaders create organizations. Also, through its optimum bringing together, deployment, and integration of the soft and hard parts, good leadership enables organizations to sustainably create their desired destinies and thrive. Without good leadership, organizations decay and atrophy as humans clash over personal interests and move aimlessly without unified actions.

Organizational design

According to N. Stanford[2], organizational design entails putting together, embedding, aligning, and interrelating the key elements of an organization, namely, its purpose, values, vision/mission, strategy/tactics, operating principles, objectives, technology/systems/ processes, structure, resources, people, culture, rewards, and performance measures, in order to sustainably deliver required results in the context of its operating environment. It therefore involves strategic thinking, planning, implementation, monitoring, control/feedback, continuous adaptation, innovation, and improvement. According to Nadler and associates [3], organizations are designed using two main perspectives: – (1) a strategy/task performance perspective that sees organizations as purely economic entities that are created to generate economic value for shareholders, customers, employees, and so on, and (2) a social/cultural perspective that sees organizations as social entities created to satisfy the social preferences, values, and aspirations of their founders/shareholders, employees, and various stakeholders. Nadler and associates argue that leaders must consider and balance both perspectives during organizational design to ensure internal/external organizational congruity and strategic fit. Organizational design is holistic and goes beyond mere restructuring, re-engineering, rightsizing, or simple systems improvement. It is guided by certain principles. According to J. R. Galbraith [4] and N. Stanford, the following are some key principles that guide organizational design or redesign:

1. A clear purpose, compelling reason, case for change, or strategic intent must be articulated for organizational design. A key adage in organizational architecture or design is "form follows function" or "structure

follows strategy"; hence, the need for clear purpose/function and strategy. This is a key leadership responsibility.

2. Design or redesign must be systemic and holistic. This means that all the key internal elements of an organization (strategy/tactics, vision/mission, values, operating principles, objectives, technology/systems/processes, structure, resources, people, culture, performance measures, rewards, etc.) and external factors (customers, community, laws/regulations, licenses, suppliers, service providers, competitions, politics/economy, etc.) that affect the organization must be considered and aligned during organizational design. Otherwise, the design may be suboptimal.

3. The organization must be encouraged and allowed to "speak." Heifetz and associates [5] liken organizations that want to improve to patients who are sick and require the attention of a medical doctor. The doctor must listen to the "patient." Consequently, organizational design should not be shrouded in mystery or secrecy, but must be open to the organization. Given that the commitment of the people in the organization will be required to "make it happen," it is advisable

to talk to relevant persons or groups who know the "pains" of the organization and to test potential "solutions" with them.
4. Organizational leaders should avoid personalizing the design. They should be less decision makers and more decision shapers during organizational design.
5. Design should be carried out with the future in mind, not just the present or immediate challenges facing the organization.
6. The design should provide alternatives or options with pros and cons for each option. This enables the design that best fits all the critical variables and strategic expectations to be chosen. Given that no design is perfect, leaders are to push for realization of the positives in the chosen design while taking steps to ameliorate the potential consequences of its downside.

According to L. A. Montuori [6] and J. R. Galbraith the key factors that enable organizations to thrive in the midst of dynamic global changes are organizational learning, creativity, and innovation; organizational trustworthiness; organizational capability; structural re-configurability and boundarylessness; strategic thinking/planning; and leadership. Given that the focus of this book is leadership/followership development (not organizational design), we will briefly look into organizational learning, creativity, innovation; and organizational trustworthiness.

Organizational learning, creativity, and innovation

Change in our current globalized world is dynamic and unpredictable. Knowledge, information, and technological advancement are moving at a fast pace. Hence, knowledge and skills obsolescence are rapid. Consequently, workers and organizations need to continuously learn to thrive. According to C. Handy, learning organizations learn as well as encourage learning [7]. He opines that some key characteristics of learning organizations include inquiry, testing, experimentation, environmental scanning, avoidance of groupthink, framing/reframing, negative capability (learning from discomforts and mistakes), caring, and encouraging all to learn.

C. Argyris asserts that learning is the detection and correction of errors.[8] Single-loop learning, which is more or less reactive learning, entails detection correction without looking into root causes, while double-loop learning entails detection, root-cause analyses, and causal correction. Interestingly, Argyris argues that higher educational qualifications tend to make people feel they know it all, which hinders continuous learning. This behavioral pattern creates internal self-defense mechanisms in some leaders and workers that prevent them from being receptive to creative ideas, feedback, and positive criticism. This makes their immediate subordinates become "yes persons," who tell them only what they want to hear. I would describe single- and double-loop learning as adaptive learning, as they tend to make corrections for events that we know or have occurred.

P. Senge [9] argues that to be creative and innovative, organizations also need to focus on generative learning, which enables them to originate and pursue new ideas and concepts that help them to overcome the vagaries of change and meet their aspired futures. Generative learning entails systems thinking, shared vision, personal mastery, team learning, and creative tension.

B. V. Oetinger asserts that organizations usually face a dilemma in their pursuit of creativity and innovation, and that is, getting rid of the old so that the new can flourish [10]. It is as if success in itself is an impediment to creativity and innovation. IBM was exemplary. Success with mainframes blinded them to the strategic growth of personal computers. Microsoft's current success with Windows applications may also blind them to new developments in consumer preferences and information technology. Consequently, unlearning and breaking loose from the past are essential to creating thriving organizations. Oetinger further opines that one way to overcome this "blindness" and inability to forget the past, is to continuously bring new people, with new eyes, into organizations and empower them to create new "unhindered" internal teams that churn out new products and services.

Overall, creating a culture that promotes organizational learning, creativity, and Innovation requires formal systems for knowledge acquisition, information interpretation, information distribution, organizational memory, and quality management. Such a culture also cherishes and promotes inquiry, testing, experimentation, environmental scanning, avoidance of groupthink, framing/reframing, negative capability (learning from discomforts and mistakes), and encouragement of the heart (even when failures occur). Leaders institute cultures; hence, leadership trustworthiness is critical to building organizations that thrive in the midst of dynamic global changes. Let's now look at organizational trustworthiness.

Organizational trustworthiness

Can two work together, unless they are agreed?
—Amos 3:3

In our current world, where organizations drop employees at will (in the name of rightsizing, downsizing, or restructuring), where the actions or inactions of organizational leaders lead to organizational failures and collapse, can employees and service providers trust organizations? The Chambers Dictionary defines trust as "worthiness to be relied upon; confident expectation from another and resting on the integrity of another." Tan and Lim define trust in organizations as "an employee's willingness to be vulnerable to the actions of the organization, whose behavior and actions he or she cannot control." According to Galford and Drapeau [12], and Tan and Lim, trust within organizations can be grouped into four categories, namely:

1. **Strategic trust**—trust in the strategies/ goals of the organization; that it is doing

the right things and it is effectively focusing its energy and resources.

2. **Process trust**—trust in the way decisions are made and the processes employed.
3. **Leadership trust**—trust in the people leading the organization.
4. **Coworker trust**—trust among coworkers who have little or no power imbalance.

Trust in organizations occurs at essentially four levels—interpersonal, team/organizational, inter-organizational, and organizational/societal levels. The key factors that contribute to organizational trust or trustworthiness are individual and organizational competence, integrity (congruence of words/promises and actions), benevolence (positive intentions toward others), and behavior/actions (for example, openness in communication, clarity of structure/roles/responsibilities, inclusiveness in decision making).

A key challenge in strategic leadership is that leaders and organizations do occasionally fail. Why do they fail and what can they do when failure occurs? The next chapter on personal and organizational renewal provides some insights.

Chapter 8

Personal and Organizational Renewal

Owing to several personal, internal, external or environmental challenges, people and organizations sometimes fail to achieve their purpose or aspirations. Some companies are now extinct because of poor strategic leadership practices. Others no longer occupy their previous top positions in the corporate world. What should individuals and companies do when they have failed or are experiencing failures? How can they change the situation and bounce back? I would argue that they require personal and organizational renewal, which usually starts with a change of values, purpose, vision and activities.

We learnt that leadership takes place at three levels—personal, team/organizational, and societal. However, leadership failures, whether at the organizational or societal levels, usually emanate from failures at the personal level. Consequently, renewal starts at the personal level.

Personal Renewal

The following Scriptures give us an inkling into how the personal renewal process starts:

> I will give you a new heart and put a new spirit within you; I will take the heart of stone out of your flesh and give you a heart of flesh. (Ezek. 36:26 NKJV)

> Therefore, If anyone is in Christ, he is a new creation; old things have passed away; behold all things have become new. (2 Cor. 5:17 NKJV)

Personal renewal goes beyond mere restoration of lost position or resources. It is a re-molding process that follows a traumatic or an unexpected experience, which is usually beyond the leader's wildest imagination. Paul's encounter with Christ during his journey to Damascus (Acts 9: 1 – 22) is exemplary; it completely changed his worldview, motives, values and activities.

It is pertinent to ask - what factors usually contribute to human beings becoming run-down (physically, emotionally, or spiritually) that they require renewal? From my experience, the key contributory factors are:

1. **Spiritual prostitution.** Spiritual prostitution entails serving idols, becoming or remaining a cult member; visiting herbalists, consulting mediums, or following false prophets, while appearing to be holy. False prophets and magical priests are similar because they cherish people entering into trouble and becoming sick, so that they can benefit from their frequent visits. Thus, they are not interested in people or organizations becoming whole or free from troubles. Spiritual prostitution usually leads to the development and use of a poor set of personal and organizational values that impair righteous decisions and practices. The Bible enjoins us to avoid spiritual prostitution. It teaches that:

    "My people are being destroyed because they don't know me. Since you priests refuse to know me, I refuse to recognize you as my priests. Since you have forgotten the laws of your God, I will forget to bless your children" (Hos. 4:6 NLT).

2. **Immorality.** Immorality is a violation of the commandments of God. It offends God and leads to poor physical health.

3. **Pride, arrogance, disobedience, and anger.** When we are carried away by power,

position, wealth, human knowledge, and uncontrolled anger, we usually derail and fail. The biblical story of Nebuchadnezzar is exemplary. He lost his kingship and became an animal because of pride. He was renewed and reinstalled back to his throne by God only after he recognized that God rules in the affairs of men and women (Dan. 4:28-37). We also learn from the Bible that "by humility and the fear of the Lord are riches and honor and life" (Prov. 22:4 NKJV). Leaders must learn to be humble and to depend on God—the true God that Jesus called His Father.

4. **Poor support base.** We cannot fight the battles of life alone. We require family members, good friends, brethren, personal confidants, coaches, colleagues and pastors to thrive. It is imperative that we cherish and not destroy our family members, friends, and support.

5. **Lack of knowledge and lack of commitment to continuously improve oneself.**
We need to continuously learn and improve ourselves in order to fulfill the biblical instruction: "Study to show thyself approved unto God, a workman that needeth not be

ashamed, rightly dividing the word of truth" (2 Tim. 2:15 KJV).

6. **Evil attacks.**

   The Bible teaches us to "be sober, be vigilant, because your adversary the devil walks about like a roaring lion, seeking whom he may devour" (1 Peter 5:8 NKJV). Consequently, we need to live righteous lives, continuously pray and seek the covering of God to avoid evil attacks.

Organizational Renewal

How does renewal take place?

Personal and organizational renewal starts when the people, especially the leaders in an organization, renew themselves.

> If My people who are called by My name will humble themselves, and pray and seek My face, and turn from their wicked ways, then I will hear from heaven, and will forgive their sins and heal their land. (2 Chron. 7:14 NKJV)

> Repent therefore and be converted, that your sins may be blotted out, so that

times of refreshing may come from the presence of the Lord. (Acts 3:19 NKJV)

The renewal process usually entails:

1. A humbling experience—brokenness, setback, unexpected adverse outcomes or failures.
2. Commitment to learn from the adverse experiences, to change and improve.
3. True repentance about things we did wrong.
4. Stoppage of actions and practices that offend God and our constituents.
5. Waiting period whilst tilling our stony hearts to change core values.
6. Following a new direction, undertaking new activities in new places.
7. Seeking God's favor, which comes at set times, to usher in the new: "You will arise and have mercy on Zion; for the time to favor her, yes the set time, has come" (Ps. 102:13 NKJV).
8. Thanksgiving and praising God for new beginnings.

How do I continue to win sustainably after renewal?

1. Develop and commit to a new purpose, mission, vision and a set of values that enable you, your organization and humanity to sustainably flourish.
2. Pursue creativity, innovation, continuous learning and improvement in all aspects of your personal and organizational lives.
3. Network and fellowship with persons and institutions that will enable you and your organization to live righteously and continuously succeed.
4. At all times, remember the biblical decree that: "the godly will flourish like palm trees and grow strong like cedars of Lebanon." (Psalm 92: 12 NLT)

I pray that you and your organization experience continuous renewal and sustainable growth as you practice the teachings in this book.

God bless you.

Dr. Mason Oghenejobo.

Endnotes

Introduction

1. Scott Roberts, *PinkNews.co.uk,* December 27, 2013, 5:55 PM.
2. Jennifer Peltz and Tom Hayes (AP) December 10, 2012 Domique Straus Kahn Settlement: Former IMF Chief, Nafissatou Diallo Settle Sexual Assault Lawsuit.
3. CNN International.Com. Politics. Clinton: Lewinsky Affair a "terrible moral error." June 21, 2004.

Chapter 1
Strategic Leadership Overview

1. Porter, M. E. (1996) *On Competition.* A Harvard Business Review Book.
2. Burgelman, R. A. *Strategy Is Destiny: How Strategy Making Shapes a Company's Future.* New York: The Free Press, 2002.

Chapter 2
Personal Leadership Poverty

1. Winston, B (2002) *Be a Leader for God's Sake.* Regent University. Virginia Beach, VA: (ISBN 0972581901).
2. Kouzes, J. M. and Posner, B. Z. (2004) *Christian Reflections on the Leadership Challenge.* Jossey Bass. USA.
3. Blanchard, K. and Hodges, P. (2005) *Lead Like Jesus.* Thomas Nelson, Inc. Tennessee. USA.
4. Rardin, R (2001) *The Servants Guide to Leadership. Beyond First Principles.* Selah Publishing USA.

5. Unglaub, K. (M.P.H.) *Rest* http://www.projectrestore.com/library/health/rest.htm
6. Cassandra, D. (2009) Is burnout claiming your firm's most productive workers? *Contractors Business Management Report 11 (Nov. 2009); 1, 14 – 15.*
7. Reichel, A., and Y. Neumann. Fall 1993. Work stress, job burnout, and work outcomes in a turbulent environment. *International Studies of Management and Organization* 23.3: 75.
8. Goleman, D. (1999) *Working with Emotional Intelligence.* Bantam Books. USA.
9. Wharton, L. (2004) Executive Health: Executive Burnout—How to recognize and beat it. *New Zealand Management (Jul 2004) 72–77.*
10. Jensen M. C. and Meckling W. H. (1976) Theory of the firm: Managerial behavior, agency costs and ownership structure. *Journal of Financial Economics.* Vol. 3, issue 4 pp. 302–360.
11. Davis, J. H., Schooman F. D. and Donaldson, L. (1997) Toward a Stewardship Theory of Management. *The Academy of Management Review.* Vol. 22. Issue 1 pp. 20–47.
12. Covey, S. R. (1992) *Principle Centred Leadership.* Simon and Schuster UK Ltd. Africa House, 64–78 Kingsway, London WC2B.
13. Kellerman, B. (2004) *Bad Leadership.* Harvard Business School Press. Boston. USA.
14. Covey, S. M. R. and Merrill, R. R. (2006) *The Speed of Trust. The One Thing that Changes Everything.* Simon and Schuster UK Ltd. Africa House, 64–78 Kingsway, London WC2B.

15. Winston, N. and Patterson, K. (2006). An integrative Definition of Leadership. *International Journal of Leadership Studies, 1(2), 6–66.*
16. Blanchard, K. et al (2007) *Leading at a Higher Level. Blanchard on Leadership and Creating High Performing Organizations.* Prentice Hall. Upper Saddle River. NJ. USA.
17. Goleman, D. et al (2002) *Primal Leadership. Realizing the Power of Emotional Intelligence.* Harvard Business School Press. Boston. USA.

Chapter 3
The Leader as Light: A Concept for Developing Global Leaders

1. Hitt, W. (1996) *A Global Ethic. The Leadership Challenge.* Batelle Press. USA.
2. Rosen, R., Digh, P., Singer, M. and Philips, C. (2000) *Global Literacies. Lessons on Business Leadership and Global Cultures.* Simon and Schuster Publishing. Rockefeller Centre, USA.
3. Black, J. S., Morrison, A. J. and Gregersen, H. B. (1999) *Global Explorers. The Next Generation of Global Leaders.* Routledge Publishers, UK.
4. Heifetz, R., Grashow, A. and Linsky, M. (2009) *The Practice of Adaptive Leadership.* Harvard Business Press.
5. Marquardt, M. and Berger, N. O. (2000) *Global Leaders for the 21st Century.* State University of New York Press.
6. Winston, B. (2002) *Be a Leader for God's Sake.* Virginia Beach, VA: Regent University. (ISBN 0972581901).

Chapter 4
Leadership Theories and Practices

1. Stogdill, R. M. (1974) *Handbook of Leadership: A Survey of Theory and Research.* New York. Free Press.
2. McCall, M. and Lombardo, M. (1983). *Off the track: Why and how successful executives get derailed* (Tech. Rep. No. 21). Greensboro, NC: Center for Creative Leadership.
3. Kouzes, J.M. and Posner, B.Z. (2004) *Christian Reflections on the Leadership Challenge.* Jossey Bass. USA.
4. Blanchard, K. et al (2007) *Leading at a Higher Level. Blanchard on Leadership and Creating High Performing Organizations.* Prentice Hall. Upper Saddle River. NJ. USA.
5. Goleman, D. et al (2002) *Primal Leadership. Realizing the Power of Emotional Intelligence.* Harvard Business School Press. Boston. USA.
6. Fieldler, F. E. (1997) *A Theory of Leadership Effectiveness.* New York. McGraw Hill.
7. Bass, B. M. and Avolio, B. J. (1994) *Improving Organizational Effectiveness Through Transformational Leadership.* Thousand Oaks, CA. USA.
8. Jensen M. C. and Meckling W. H. (1976) Theory of the firm: Managerial behavior, agency costs and ownership structure. *Journal of Financial Economics.* Vol. 3, issue 4 pp. 302–360.
9. Davis, J. H., Schooman F. D. and Donaldson, L. (1997) Toward a Stewardship Theory of Management. *The Academy of Management Review.* Vol. 22. Issue 1 pp. 20–47.

Chapter 5
Power and Influence

1. French, J. and Raven, B. H. (1959) The bases of social power. *Ann Arbor, MI: Institute for Social Research.*
2. Bass, B. M. (1960) *Leadership, Psychology and Organizational Behavior.* Harper. New York.
3. Yukl, G. (2002) Leadership in Organizations. *Fifth Edition.* Prentice Hall. NJ. USA.

Chapter 6
Coaching, Counseling, Mentoring, and Discipling

1. Rubin, Hank (2009). *Collaborative Leadership: Developing Effective Partnerships for Communities and Schools.* Corwin Press.
2. Bell. C. R. (2002) *Managers as Mentors,* Berrett-Koehler Publishers, Inc. San Francisco, CA, USA.

Chapter 7
Organizational Theories and Practices

1. Morgan, G. (1998) *Images of Organization. The Executive Edition.* Berret-Koehler Publishers, Inc. San Francisco. USA.
2. Stanford, N. (2007) *Guide to Organizational Design.* The Economist in Association with Profile Books. London. UK.
3. Nadler, D. A., Gerstein, M. S. and Shaw, R. B. (1992) *Organizational Architecture: Designs for Changing Organizations.* Jossey Bass Publishers. San Francisco.
4. Galbraith, J. R. (2002) *Designing Organizations. An Executive Guide to Strategy, Structure and Process.* Jossey Bass. USA.

5. Heifetz, R., Grashow, A. and Linsky, M. (2009) *The Practice of Adaptive Leadership*. Harvard Business Press.
6. Montuori, L. A. (2000) Organizational Longevity: Integrating systems thinking, learning and conceptual complexity. *Journal of Organizational Change Management,* Vol 13 No. 1, pp. 61–73.
7. Handy, C. (1989) *The age of unreason*. Boston. Harvard Business School Press.
8. Argyris, C. (1993) *Knowledge for Action. A guide to overcoming barriers to organizational change.* Jossey Bass. San Francisco. USA.
9. Senge: http://www.infed.org/thinkers/senge.htm.
10. Oetinger, B. V. (2004) From Idea to Innovation. Making Creativity Real. *Journal of Business Strategy.* Vol. 25 no. 5 2004 pp. 35–41, Emerald Group Publishing Limited. ISSN 0275-6668.
11. Tan H. H. and Lim A. K. (2009) Trust in Coworkers and Trust in Organizations. *The Journal of Psychology*, 143(1), 45–66.
12. Galford, R. and Drapeau, S. (2002) *The Trusted Leader.* The Free Press. New York. USA

About the Author

Dr. Mason Oghenejobo has a B.Sc in Petroleum Engineering from the University of Ibadan, Nigeria; Masters of Business Administration (M.B.A) from Webster University, Leiden, Netherlands; Certificate of Professional Development (CPD) with emphasis in business strategy from the Wharton Business School, University of Pennsylvania, Philadelphia, USA; Certificate of Advanced Graduate Studies (CAGS) in Organisational Leadership and Doctor of Strategic Leadership (DSL) from Regent University, Virginia Beach, USA. He is also an alumnus of the Lagos Business School Senior Management Programme and the University of Oxford Advanced Management and Leadership Programme.

He worked with Shell for about 32 years in various capacities, which included Area Manager – Land East, GM Commercial, Director of OK LNG, Director of Shell Nigeria Gas and the Vice President Security. He is currently a strategy, leadership development and organizational development/renewal consultant. He is the Founder/Chairman of the Better Than Gold Institute (www.btgiglobal.com), a non-profit Christian organization dedicated to raising righteous leaders across the world.

He is married to Mrs. Vivian Oghenejobo and they are blessed with children and grandchildren.

Email contact: masogh@yahoo.com

www.ingramcontent.com/pod-product-compliance
Lightning Source LLC
Chambersburg PA
CBHW021544200526
45163CB00015B/1236